A Note to Parents

D1054731

DK READERS is a compelling program for beginning readers, designed in conjunction with leading literacy experts, including Dr. Linda Gambrell, Professor of Education at Clemson University. Dr. Gambrell has served as President of the National Reading Conference and the College Reading Association, and has recently been elected to serve as President of the International Reading Association.

Beautiful illustrations and superb full-color photographs combine with engaging, easy-to-read stories and informational texts to offer a fresh approach to each subject in the series. Each DK READER is guaranteed to capture a child's interest while developing his or her reading skills, general knowledge, and love of reading.

The five levels of DK READERS are aimed at different reading abilities, enabling you to choose the books that are exactly right for your child:

Pre-level 1: Learning to read
Level 1: Beginning to read
Level 2: Beginning to read alone
Level 3: Reading alone
Level 4: Proficient readers

The "normal" age at which a child begins to read can be anywhere from three to eight years old. Adult participation through the lower levels is very helpful for providing encouragement, discussing storylines, and sounding out unfamiliar words.

No matter which level you select, you can be sure that you are helping your child learn to read, then read to learn!

LONDON, NEW YORK,
MELBOURNE, MUNICH, AND DELHI

Project Editor Laura Gilbert
Designer Jon Hall
Brand Manager Lisa Lanzarini
Publishing Manager Simon Beecroft
Category Publisher Siobhan Williamson
Production Nick Seston
DTP Designer Santosh Kumar G

Lucasfilm
Executive Editor Jonathan W. Rinzler
Art Director Troy Alders
Continuity Supervisor Leland Chee

Reading Consultant
Linda B. Gambrell, Ph.D.

First published in the United States in 2007
by DK Publishing,
375 Hudson Street
New York, New York 10014

08 09 10 11 10 9 8 7 6 5 4 3

SD354—8/07

Copyright © 2007 Lucasfilm Ltd. and ™.
All rights reserved. Used under authorization.
Page design copyright © 2007 Dorling Kindersley Limited

All rights reserved under International and Pan-American
Copyright Conventions. No part of this publication may be
reproduced, stored in a retrieval system, or transmitted in any form
or by any means, electronic, mechanical, photocopying, recording,
or otherwise, without the prior written permission of the copyright
owner. Published in Great Britain by Dorling Kindersley Limited.

A catalog record for this book is available from the Library of Congress.

ISBN: 978-0-7566-3274-8 (Paperback)
ISBN: 978-0-7566-3275-5 (Hardback)

Color reproduction by Wyndeham Pre-Press Ltd., UK
Printed and bound in China by L Rex Printing Co., Ltd.

Discover more at
www.dk.com

www.starwars.com

DK READERS

STAR WARS

READY, SET, PODRACE!

BEGINNING **1** TO READ

Written by Simon Beecroft

Do you like fast races?

Would you like to see
the fastest race ever?

A Podrace is the fastest race
you will ever see!

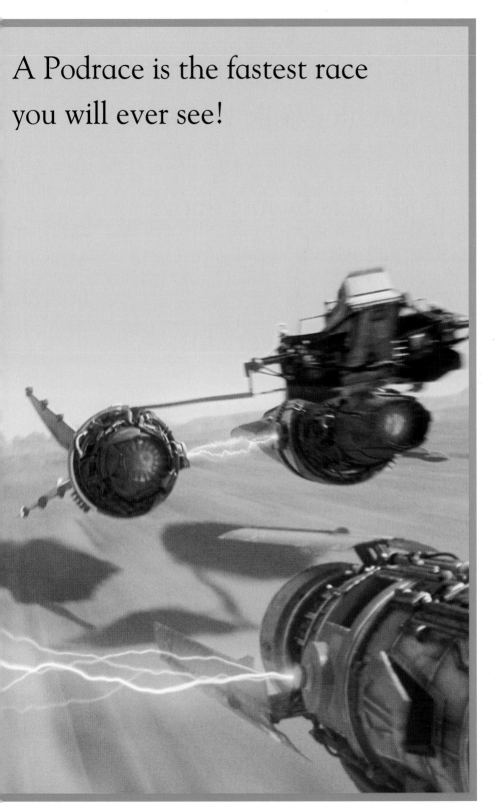

In a Podrace, each pilot flies
a machine called a Podracer.

Podracers fly just above
the ground.

Podracers fly very fast!

Podracer

Podracer pilots sit
in a seat called
a cockpit.

Cockpit

All the driving controls
are in front of them.

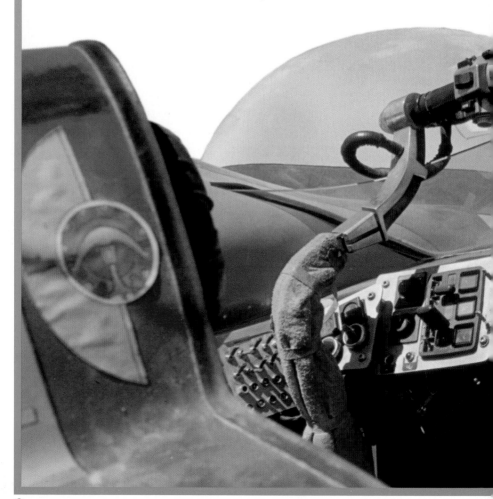

The pilots have to move
the controls very quickly
when they are racing.

Do you think you could fly
a Podracer?

This desert racetrack has lots of twists and turns.
Some of these twists and turns are very dangerous.

The pilot who
reaches the end
of the race first
is the winner.

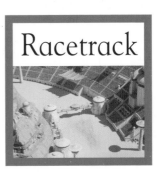

Racetrack

Many people come to watch
the Podraces.
The people shout and cheer.

They are excited to see the race.
They want to find out
which racer will win.

Podracing is very dangerous.

The pilots fly along at really fast speeds.

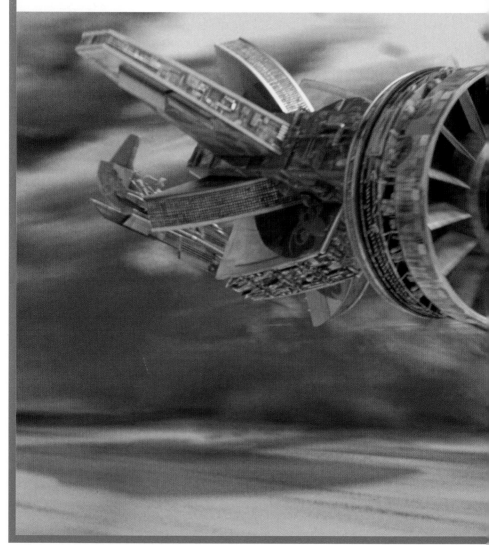

Some racers crash into each other, and some racers crash into cliffs.

Pilots often look quite unusual.

This pilot has four arms and two legs. He uses all of his four arms while he races.

This pilot has three eyes.
His extra eye helps him
spot dangers in the race.

This pilot is wearing goggles.
They are special racing goggles.
His racing goggles
protect his eyes
from the desert sand.

This pilot is nervous.
He is worried because
his Podracer is broken.
He will not finish the race.

This pilot is named Sebulba (pronounced SA-BULL-BAH). He cheats in the race in order to win.

He also cheats because he is not very nice.

Sebulba sometimes throws
his tools at the
other pilots.
He wants to
force them out
of the race.

Tools

Selbulba is a very
dangerous
racer.

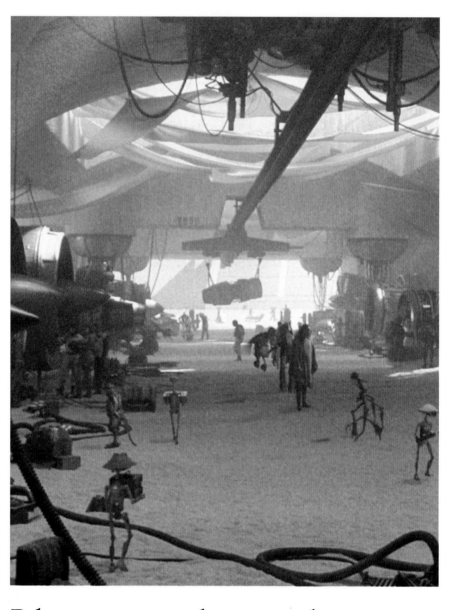

Pilots prepare their machines
for the race in a big garage
called a hangar.

Robots clean
the Podracers and
repair the engines.

Each pilot makes
sure his Podracer
is ready to go!

Engines

Today is one of the most exciting Podraces ever.

It is exciting because one of the racers is a young boy. The boy is named Anakin (AN-NA-KIN).

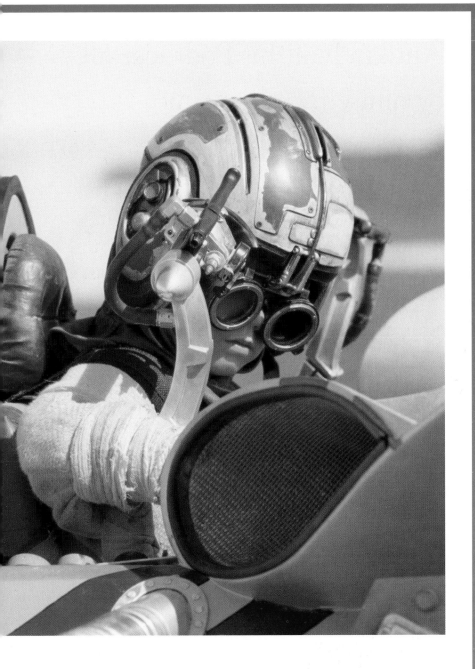

Anakin has never finished
a Podrace before.

Anakin built his Podracer all by himself.

He is only nine years old,
but he is a very good pilot.

Anakin's family and friends are
going to watch him race.

The pilots are on the starting line.
Ready, set,
Podrace!

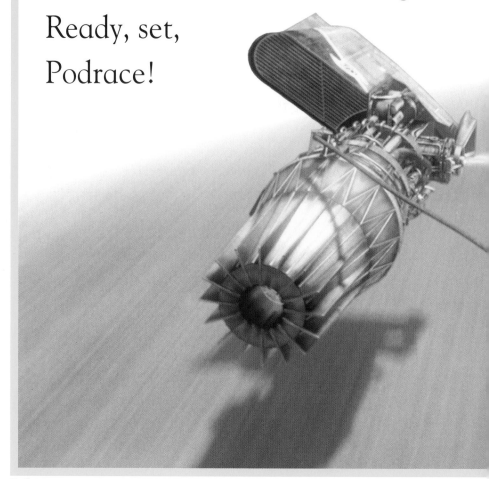

The race is very exciting.
Sebulba does everything he can
to win.
He tries to push Anakin out
of the race.

Anakin is a better racer
than Sebulba.
Sebulba crashes!

Anakin wins the race.
Anakin's friends and family are
very happy, but Anakin is
happiest of all!

Glossary

 Cockpit a space that a pilot sits in

 Engines machines that make a vehicle move

 Podracer a vehicle that flies close to the ground

 Racetrack an oval piece of track that vehicles race on

 Tools items that are used for mechanical work